We dedicate this book with love
to everyone's mother—
Mother Earth,
And to all mothers, who, with unbounded
generosity, Create, nourish and sustain life
And fill our world with beauty and love.

Contents

Introduction

There is no one like a mother. Our mothers give us life, love us, take care of us and want the best for us, no matter how old we are. There is no way to adequately describe the gift they have given us.

No other experience in the world compares to being a mother. Being pregnant, going through labor and childbirth, and for both adoptive and biological mothers, seeing your baby's face for the very first time—these powerful occurrences are just the start of the unique role in life we call motherhood.

How can we ever adequately thank our mothers for the gift of life and unconditional love? How can we honor our daughters, wives, friends and other relatives who are mothers for the enormously important job they do? We can remember to express all the love and gratitude we feel for them. We at Chicken Soup offer this "bouquet of stories" to mothers, and their children, everywhere. We hope it will warm your heart, make you laugh and give mothers a renewed sense of purpose and courage to continue what so many feel is life's most rewarding—and challenging—occupation.

Growing Up

Children are the anchors that hold a mother to life.

SOPHOCLES

My mother had been reading me the story of *The Borrowers*, tiny visitors who hid in the nooks and crannies of a house. Captivated, I had set up a tiny dining room under a bookcase with dollhouse furniture. For weeks, I'd left out crumbs and a little bowl of water—the cap of the ketchup bottle—before I went to bed. Each morning before school, I would check to see if the Borrowers had returned. The water and crumbs would be gone. Sometimes there would even be a minuscule thank-you note left for me.

At nine, I should probably have been too old to really believe in the Borrowers. And though I suspected that my tiny visitors might be my mother's doing, I still held on to my belief that they just might be real. Then one day I came home from school, and my mother was gone. So were the Borrowers.

"Mommy is very sick," my father said to me, his usually bright blue eyes looking tired and sad. "She's going to be in the hospital for a while until she gets better. Her kidneys aren't working right, and the doctors are going to make her better, but it's going to be a few weeks until you can see her because the doctors need that time to fix everything, okay?"

At first it seemed almost like a holiday. Everyone was especially nice to me; my father made my favorite meals or we would go out to dinner. He would bring home letters from my mother, "Make sure you ask Daddy to help you brush your hair; once the knots start, they are so hard to brush out." My hair, fine and wavy, was prone to tangles.

"Why can't I go and see Mommy?" I would ask him.

But his answer was always the same, "Not yet. She's too weak right now . . . but soon."

It was difficult to imagine my mother weak. We went swimming together every day in the summer, walking the five or so miles to the community pool and back again. Sometimes we chased each other around the house playing tag until the downstairs neighbors became so aggravated they would bang on the ceiling for us to stop. Then we'd collapse on the floor from laughing so hard, each of us trying in vain to be quiet.

And no matter how busy she was, she always had enough time to sit on the floor and play dolls with me. In her games, my dolls were never just going to parties, they were architects or doctors, or even running for Congress! I was probably the only nine-year-old whose mother introduced her to *Jane Eyre* and *Gone with the Wind*. I would read a bit of the book each day, and we would sit and discuss it over tea and cookies.

"The women in these books are strong, Lisa. They go through very difficult situations and learn that they can take care of themselves," my mother would tell me. She admired the strength in Jane and Scarlett, and she wanted me to value it as well.

But then things had begun to change. More often I would get up in the morning to fix my own breakfast, or come home from school to find a neighbor waiting to bring me to her home after school. Sometimes my parents would be in their bedroom talking with the door closed. The day the Borrowers stopped coming, I knew something was really wrong.

With my mother gone, I noticed that my father rarely went into my parents' bedroom anymore. I'd sometimes get up in the middle of night and find him lying asleep on the couch in the flickering light of the television, still in his work clothes. Pulling the blanket up over him and turning off the TV, I was a girl who was growing up. A girl who no longer believed in the Borrowers.

"Daddy?" I asked my father one day, "Is Mommy going to die?" He looked at me for what seemed forever, then grabbed my arms and pulled me to him. "Maybe," he said and then lowered his head and began to weep. I wrapped my arms around his neck and held him close. We sat there and cried, for the first time, together.

Then he told me that my mother had been diagnosed with end-stage renal failure, which meant that her kidneys had failed and that unless she had a kidney transplant, she would probably die. In the early 1970s, dialysis as a treatment for renal failure was in its early stages. My mother was at the County Medical Center where they had access to new medical technology. It had been touch-and-go for several weeks, and at times it appeared as though they might have waited too long to be able to help my mother. I told my father I wanted to see her.

At the hospital, my father shouted at the nurse at the desk in the intensive care unit, "I don't care if it's not allowed."

"It will be too disturbing for the child," the nurse said to my dad in a low voice, motioning for him to lower his voice as well.

My father walked over to me where I was sitting on a bench against the wall. "Listen, Honey, I'm going to go and talk to the chief of staff about you seeing your mommy. Sit here and draw me a picture, and I'll be back in a few minutes, okay?" I nodded my head and watched him walk off down the hall with the nurse.

The large double doors had the words "Only Medical Staff Allowed" written on them in large bold letters. A sign in front of the bench said "Children under fifteen not admitted." The sounds coming from behind the double doors frightened me and the thought that my mother was in there frightened me even more.

But as I sat there, my fear dissolved and I became angrier and angrier. Who were these strangers to keep me away from my mother? Scarlett O'Hara wouldn't have sat by and let people tell her what she could and couldn't do. My mother was behind that door, and I was going to go in and find her.

Putting both hands on one side of the ICU door, I pushed as hard as I could. Inside, bright fluorescent lights illuminated the room, people in white scurried around and loud beeping filled the air. Without knowing how I knew, I turned to my right and started to walk toward a bed where most of the activity was being focused. No one seemed to notice me.

The woman on the bed seemed very

small and was surrounded by tubes and machines with blinking lights. She looked like my mother, except paler and smaller than I remembered. Her eyes were closed and her long dark hair was spread out on her pillow.

"She's not responding!" a white-coated man shouted. "Her pressure is too low," a nurse shouted back to the man in the white coat.

"Mommy," I said quietly, then again louder. "Mommy?"

People started running over to me. "Get her out of here!" bellowed the man in the white coat.

"Wait!" shouted the nurse and motioned for me to come over. As I walked over to my mother, everyone stepped back except for the man in the white coat who tried to grab my shoulder. The nurse standing by the bed put her hand up to stop him.

"Look," she said, glancing down at my mother.

My mother had opened her eyes. "Lisa?" She turned her head to look at me and smiled. The frenetic beeping seemed to slow down.

"Mommy, it's me." I stood next to the bed,

wanting to crawl in beside her despite the machines and tubes all around her.

"Come here." She raised her arms, and I let her wrap her arms around me. "Don't be scared by all of this. These machines are going to make me better. We'll have one in our house, and I'll be able to come home to stay." Frowning ever so slightly, she added, "Has anyone been helping you brush your hair?" Laughter from behind me reminded me that we weren't alone. Doctors and nurses were standing around watching us, many with tears in their eyes.

They knew, though I didn't, that only moments ago my mother had actually died. Later she told me that she remembered seeing a young woman lying on a hospital bed connected to tubes and machines. She felt very sorry for the woman until she realized that she was looking at herself and, for the first time in months, she felt no pain or discomfort. In what seemed like a movie, she remembered seeing people rush over to her to try and resuscitate her.

"I felt such peace, such happiness. I didn't want to be that woman on the bed anymore until I heard a girl's voice that said 'Mommy?'"

When she realized that the voice was mine, she knew that she had to come back. I'm sure that if I hadn't violated hospital policy and been there to call her back, things would have turned out very differently.

Soon after, my mother came home, along with a dialysis machine that became a permanent part of our family. And although the Borrowers never returned, I didn't need them anymore. I was a girl who could brush the tangles out of her own hair. I could fix a meal or two without any help. I was a girl who still had her mother. And that was the most important part.

Lisa Duffy-Korpics

Mother of Three Thousand Sons

Who gives to me teaches me to give.

ANCIENT PROVERB

Thirty years ago, when I was a journalist in Philadelphia, I founded a small magazine called Umoja (Swahili for unity), which dealt with the issues confronting African-Americans.

Because of the many letters the magazine received about the gang problem in our city, I asked my husband, Dave, to do some research. He began walking the streets, asking questions, talking to people and observing the problem firsthand.

My interest in the subject was purely

professional—until the day Dave returned from a fact-finding mission and reported that our second son, Robin, was a member of a gang. Even worse, Robin was the gang's favorite, called the "heart of the corner." The heart is the favorite target if gang wars occur. I was shocked and frightened. How could this be happening in my home, in my family? But it was true. My son was a walking bull's-eye.

We had six sons, ranging in age from eleven to eighteen. I looked carefully at sixteen-year-old Robin that evening when he came home. I hadn't noticed it before, but Robin was different. He wore his clothing differently, and his manner was tougher. I confronted him, and he didn't lie. Yes, he was a gang member—and nothing I said or did was going to change that.

It was as if the bottom dropped out of my world. I stopped eating; I couldn't sleep. In an effort to save my son, I talked to social service agencies and the police, but no one seemed to have an answer. No one seemed able to do anything.

But everyone agreed that the breakdown of the family was the main source of the gang problem. I thought our family was strong, but for Robin, obviously something was missing.

Then an idea came to me. If family was the problem, could family also be the solution? Why not invite Robin's gang to live in our home? We could show them how real families work.

"Are you out of your mind?" Dave said when I told him my idea.

But I was on fire with my idea and wouldn't give up. Eventually he agreed to give it a try. Our other sons were more or less open—they knew Robin's life was on the line. Robin was thrilled with the idea— his boys and his family all under one roof.

Robin's gang leader, in serious trouble on the street, needed a place to hide out. He jumped at the chance to live with us, and the rest of the gang followed his lead. I called every parent I could reach to inform them of our plan, and they all agreed to let their sons come to us.

Our house was a small one, hardly large enough for our original family. When fifteen more boys moved in, it felt as crowded as a sardine can. But we made it work. All the boys slept in sleeping bags on the living room floor, and at mealtime the sleeping bags were rolled and stowed and folding tables and chairs were set up.

The first few weeks were difficult. Many times I wondered if Dave had been right about me being out of my mind. The boys chafed at doing chores, wouldn't participate in our family meetings and didn't want to get the part-time jobs I insisted on. But I was determined. I looked at the situation as if it were a puzzle and knew we'd have to find the right pieces if we were going to save the lives of these kids.

Finally we asked the boys to devise rules we could all live by. We were a little nervous about this because if we didn't like their rules, it would be difficult to enforce our own. But I breathed a sigh of relief when they read out their four rules: 1) No fighting in the house, 2) No drugs or drinking, 3) No girls in their rooms, and 4) No gang warring.

Maybe, just maybe, this will work, I thought. We found that since the boys had made up the rules, they were very good about keeping them.

The biggest and most pressing challenge

was getting enough food. Our small savings were soon exhausted, but I had the idea to sell back issues of the magazine, Umoja, that were stored in our basement. The boys took stacks and peddled them all over Philadelphia, bringing home money to buy food.

We also approached a local church and told them we needed food. They were very supportive and sent notices to affluent parishes asking for food donations. The response was overwhelming. Soon we were inundated. Trucks loaded with food began coming down our block, headed for "The House of Umoja."

Now we had more food than we could use. We decided to give some away to people in the area who could use it. The boys were excited about distributing food. For most of them, it was the first time they had ever found themselves in the position of benefactors—giving something to help others.

After that, things began to fall into place. The boys got jobs and began contributing money to cover our household expenses. This new "gang" organized yard sales, sold candy door-to-door, and escorted elderly people to the bank.

We faced our largest hurdle the day George, one of the old gang's bitterest rivals, showed up asking to join our family. He realized he needed to take this drastic step, or he would end up in jail or dead. The boys were silent, wrestling with their hatred for their former enemy. But something new had entered their hearts—commitment to family, compassion, kindness—squeezing out their old "turf mentality." The tension broke as the boys accepted George into our new family.

As the weeks went by, I found myself falling in love with the boys; they became like my own children. Some of them even started calling me Mom. When the gang had first arrived, they'd all had street names like Killer, Snake Eyes, Bird, Crow and Peewee. I began to give them African names with special meanings. These were names that acknowledged their bravery or discipline or strength. Although it was never stated, the boys knew they had to earn those names.

Stories about our family spread all over the city. More and more boys came wanting to live with us. Finally, the state of Pennsylvania offered us a contract to officially care for these boys under the banner of foster care. We became "House of Umoja–Boystown," and with our new funds, we were able to expand, buying more houses on our street and hiring staff. The flow of boys kept coming . . . and we just kept opening our arms to gather them in.

It wasn't always easy living with these street kids. Most people had given up on them, and for good reason. Everyone else told these boys what to do, but I decided to listen to them instead. I tried always to see them through a mother's eyes, focusing on the good in them. It didn't always work, but enough of the time, it did.

It didn't work with one boy named Spike. From the first moment he arrived he was a troublemaker—picking fights, refusing to work, disrupting meetings. When he left, I shook my head in despair. I had tried so hard to show him what it felt like to be a member of a loving family. I hated to lose any of the boys.

Some years later, a man came bursting into my office with a baby in his arms. It was Spike! "Mom," he said, placing his tiny daughter in my arms, "I want you to give her a name."

I was speechless with surprise, but as I looked at the beautiful child in my arms, her name came to me: "Fatima," I said softly, "it means 'Shining One.'"

Spike took Fatima from me and said, "I want to raise her like you showed me. I want her to be part of our family." Spike had heard me after all.

There have been other boys, too, who have surprised me by the depth of their dedication and commitment to our family. Two years after we started our experiment, we decided to have a gang conference. We asked the kids who lived with us, as well as the young men who had gone on to careers and their own homes, to go back to their old gangs and ask the new leaders to come to the conference to discuss ending gang deaths citywide. When one boy approached his old gang, they beat him up so badly he ended up in the hospital for a few days. But the minute he was released, that boy went straight back and again asked the gang leader if he would come to our house for the conference. Out of respect for his bravery, the gang leader attended.

Those were the first boys. In the thirty years since, over three thousand have followed. They are all my sons. Though some are now middle-aged men, they still come back to the house for advice or just to visit, play basketball and talk to the current group of young men who make up the family at the House of Umoja. They often bring their wives and children to celebrate birthdays and anniversaries.

I began with only the intention to save my son's life, but that simple act of motherly love grew, blossoming into a full-time service that has saved thousands of lives. While no one person can do everything, anyone can start something.

Unity, love, family—these are the things that saved my sons and will save many more sons to come. There is no limit to this love. My own name, Falaka, means "new day." Every day for me is another opportunity to be a mother to these boys who, more than anything, simply need love.

Falaka Fattah

Confessions of a Stepmother

Accept the things to which fate binds you, and love the people with whom fate brings you together, but do so with all your heart.

MARCUS AURELIUS

When I met Larry, my husband-to-be, he came complete with an eighteen-month-old daughter, McKenna, and a four-year-old son, Lorin—on weekends.

The day I met the children, we walked around a pond, Larry holding the diapered McKenna in his arms while Lorin ran around finding frogs to show me. I was stunned. These children were an enormous piece of the man I loved and yet had really nothing to do with me. How did this stepmother thing work?

I quickly fell in love with Lorin's impish grin and McKenna's pudgy baby body, warm against my chest as I held her. I was completely captivated by my new and charming "instant family," but the children's mother, Dia, was a different story. We had a wary relationship, the edge of hostility between us only thinly veiled. I did my best to ignore her and focused instead on the two adorable children she'd borne.

The children and I got along well, though Lorin was somewhat standoffish. Perhaps it was loyalty to his mother, or being a boy, or at four simply wanting more independence. McKenna, being so little, had no such qualms. She loved me and let me know it, unreservedly and with a sweetness and innocence that took my breath away. I couldn't resist her love and when I fell, I fell hard. Almost immediately, we formed our own mutual fan club—two hearts that beat as one.

In fact, it was McKenna who proposed to me first. We sat together in an airport waiting room, on our way to visit Larry's parents. She was almost three, and she sat facing me in my lap, playing with my necklace and every so often looking into my face with

worshipful eyes. I smiled at her, feeling the
fullness of love for her present in my own
heart. Larry sat beside us and Lorin was
motoring around the rows of plastic seats,
making engine noises with his mouth. To the
casual observer, a typical young family. But
we weren't a family because Larry hadn't
popped the question yet. And although I
didn't want to be pushy, we both knew my
patience was wearing thin. What, I wondered, was he waiting for?

Then McKenna pulled her pacifier out of
her mouth and returning my smile, said
brightly, "Will you marry me?" After a
moment of shocked silence, we all laughed
till our sides hurt. Me with delight, Larry
with the release of tension and the children
simply because the grown-ups were laughing. Happily, it didn't take Larry long to follow up with his own proposal.

As time went on, I got used to part-time
parenting—and having the children's mother
as an unavoidable part of my life. I really liked
Dia, but our positions seemed to dictate a certain grumpiness with each other that I did
my best to squelch. Sometimes I had the
guilty wish that the children's mother would

simply disappear. A quick and painless illness and on her deathbed, she would make me promise to raise her children for her. Then the children could stay with us—truly be mine— and we could be a "real" family.

Fortunately that never happened. I didn't really want her to die; I just was jealous that she'd had children with my husband. All right, so he was her husband at the time—it still rankled.

I watched the children grow, changing from toddlers to schoolkids. And their mother and I continued our civilized and awkward interactions, arranging for the children to come and go and negotiating vacations and holiday schedules.

My friends all told me that Larry should deal with his ex-wife, and for a while we tried that. But as an active and willing caregiver, I was involved with decisions, so Dia and I went back to our previous arrangement. And as the years went by, I noticed that our phone calls changed. I actually enjoyed talking to Dia about the kids. And I think she realized that there were very few people in the world who were as interested in, charmed by or concerned about her children as I was. We began a slow but perceptible metamorphosis that was completed the year Dia sent me a Mother's Day card, thanking me for "co-mothering" her children.

That was the beginning of a new era for Dia and me. And while it hasn't always been perfect, I know now it's been extraordinary. I have a few thank-yous of my own:

Thank you, Dia, for being big enough to share your children with me. If you hadn't, I would never have known what it was like to hold a sleeping infant and feel the complete trust displayed in the limp, silky-skinned limbs gathered carefully in my embrace. I wouldn't have had the opportunity to marvel at the twists and turns a little boy's mind makes as he tries to make sense of a large and complex universe.

I would never have known that children could cry so loudly when their stomachs hurt or that after they threw up, they could smile so radiantly at you, the tears still wet on their cheeks, their pain already forgotten.

I would never have watched a boy struggle to become his own person, or have been so closely involved with the painful and serious process of "growing a teenager." I would never have had the awe-inspiring privilege of watching that squirty twelve-year-old who could drive you wild with his questions turn into a heartbreakingly handsome hunk with the megawatt smile and charming personality. As he gets ready to leave for college, I know he will drive a new generation of women wild—for entirely different reasons.

I wouldn't have felt the thrill of seeing our beautiful daughter on stage, expressing herself with a grace and depth of emotion that seemed too old for someone so young. Or had the distinctly undeserved (and guilty) thrill of vanity and pride when someone who didn't know us commented that McKenna looked like me.

Thank you for making Christmas morning a communal occasion, so the children never had to feel divided on the holiday they held so dear. I looked around one year as we all sat around the tree, while the children delivered the gifts. There we were, you and your husband, Larry and me, the kids . . . and surprisingly, I felt at home.

I understood then that you didn't have to disappear for us to be a real family.

Carol Kline

"Wait, Dear, you don't have
to run away; I will."

A Letter to My Baby

Suddenly she was here. And I was no longer pregnant; I was a mother. I never believed in miracles before.

ELLEN GREENE

I waited, staring blankly around the white sterile examining room. The nurse had said she would be right back with the test results, but the minutes dragged by. I sat with only a single white sheet covering me, waiting for what turn my life might take. The cold, plastic-cushioned table was becoming uncomfortable, but it did not distract me enough to pull my attention elsewhere. All my thoughts centered around one question. "What if . . . ?"

What if . . . I am pregnant? What will I do? How will I support myself and a baby? These thoughts were interrupted by what felt like the fluttering of butterflies inside my stomach as the door swept open. The nurse entered; I searched her face, but it was empty of expression. When she began to speak, her voice was flat, a dreary monotone. Though I did not catch her words, I knew exactly what she was telling me: I was pregnant.

I didn't say anything, but just sat still, gazing dully at her pasty complexion. There were no encouraging words offered, no squeeze of a hand. Water welled up in my eyes, and I no longer saw or heard anything. I wrapped my arms around myself and wept.

Thoughts and tears both came rushing: I couldn't take care of myself very well. I was always worried about money. Now I was supposed to care and nurture a tiny human being? It scared me so much to think I had been stupid enough to get pregnant. The tears came even faster now. I huddled in my new reality. I was going to have a baby.

The months passed, and as my body

grew, so did my fears. I felt so utterly ill-equipped for the business of being a mom. Especially a single mom.

During that time, I talked to friends who did their best to encourage me. I spoke to a counselor once a week. I went swimming every Thursday with another pregnant woman I knew. But most often, when I wasn't working, I sat in front of the television, trying not to think about what would happen after the baby was born.

One day, close to my due date, I sat in my usual spot on my futon couch watching soap opera after soap opera, waiting for the arrival of my daughter, Loreena. (I had picked out her name as soon as I found out she was a girl.) Then it was time for my favorite talk show. The show that day was about parenting. One woman read a letter written to her by her daughter before the daughter had passed away. Though the tears streamed down the mother's face as she read, it obviously brought her great joy and comfort to see the loving words her daughter had set down on paper for her mom.

I was immediately inspired to write to my unborn daughter. Suddenly, it was the most important thing in the world to let her know—on paper—that I would always love her and cherish her and that I would do my best to make up for the absence of a father in her life. When Loreena first moved inside of me, I had realized she was "real." But as I watched the TV show, it was the first time that I thought of Loreena as a person, with her own needs and wants, rather than "the baby I would have to care for somehow."

I was excited to write to her. I waddled over to my desk and got out my stationery. I sat to write, pen poised above the paper. I closed my eyes for a moment, connecting to Loreena, wondering how to say what was in my heart. Opening my eyes, I began to write.

Dear Loreena,   *4–8–99*

Here we are, waiting for your arrival. I go through all your tiny outfits and dream about the day when we will meet in the outside world. I know you already, my baby. I know you are strong and stubborn. Each kick and flutter announces, "Hey Mom. Here I am!" Our bond is strong now, but it will be even stronger when I can show you my love and we can build our relationship, day by day.

*I have been very frightened about having
you by myself, but over these months I have
grown to cherish your every movement and
have anticipated the day we touch, skin on
skin.*

*You are and always will be my angel. I
thank God that you are a part of my life.*

Love,
Mother

I smiled as I folded the stationery into the
envelope and sealed it. I reached down on
the floor beside my bed and picked up the
keepsake box I'd created for my little
daughter-to-be. I placed the envelope in the
box, then closed it. When the lid snapped
shut, it was as if I closed away all my fears,
too. All that remained were thoughts of
Loreena joining me soon.

Twenty days later, Loreena entered the
world. I didn't sleep at all for the entire
twenty-four hours I stayed in the hospital. I
couldn't tear my eyes away from the tiny
creature who had changed my existence.
My daughter, my little angel, was perfect. I
didn't want to miss anything.

Today, it's hard to remember those fears I
had. They've disappeared, replaced by the

feeling that being Loreena's mom is the most natural thing in the world.

My daughter is already a year old. She's outgrown the tiny outfits and booties I first dressed her in, and I've put them away in her keepsake box, along with presents people have given her for "when she's older."

Each time I tuck another treasure in the box, I see the envelope addressed in my handwriting to Loreena. I envision the day years from now when my daughter is able to read and will open that envelope and see the words of love I wrote—on the day I was finally ready to be a mom.

Karie L. Hansen

Race Against Time

*To maintain a joyful family requires much
from both the parents and the children. Each
member of the family has to become, in a
special way, the servant of others.*

POPE JOHN PAUL II

The back legs on the chair almost lifted off
the floor as Clarin leaned closer to the television screen—closer to the image that tugged
at her heart.

"Anna," the voice said in a Russian accent.
The voice said something more, and the
little girl obeyed: She danced a little, sang a
little. Then the tape stopped. "She only has a
few months," the woman beside Clarin said.
"A few months before she's lost for good . . ."

We can't let that happen, Clarin thought. But can we stop it in time?

Just weeks earlier, Clarin and her husband Paul hadn't even heard of the little Russian girl. Their life was full raising six kids. The oldest, Josh, was leaving for college. The youngest, Stephen, still needed his boo-boos kissed. In between, there were pleas to borrow the car from Allyson and Brian, seventeen and sixteen, and pleas for privacy from Kristal and Alex, thirteen and ten.

Then one day, Clarin's friend Michelle, who'd adopted a Russian boy, told Clarin about Anna.

"She's a loving girl—and blind," Michelle said, as the couples sat around in the May sun.

Blind? Clarin's heart ached. Anna had been in the orphanage since birth. And though she'd been well cared for, it was still far from being a real home. And if they didn't find a home for her by the time she turned seven in November, "they'll transfer her to a home for invalids. And those places are awful—the neglect, the abuse. . . . " Michelle sighed.

Later that evening, Clarin couldn't stop thinking about Anna. Years before, hearing heartbreaking stories about orphans in other countries, the couple had considered foreign adoption. But as their own children came along, those plans had faded—until now.

"What if we adopted Anna?" she said, taking Paul's hand.

He'd been thinking the same thing. But how could they afford it on Paul's salary as a teacher, and Clarin a stay-at-home mom? She felt her heart sink, but the thought came, What if one of my kids had to live in that dark, distant world? And in just a few months' time, that world would turn more frightening—and cruel.

But this wasn't a decision she and Paul could make alone. "It will affect your lives, too," Clarin explained to the kids. "Search your hearts."

It would mean sharing everything with one more. But this little girl had nothing. Before long, the children had an answer: "Bring her home."

And now as they sat in the adoption agency, watching the videotape of a little girl auditioning for someone to want her, Clarin knew just how important this mission was.

Many in the invalid homes die from illness, Clarin learned. And if Anna does survive there, Clarin was told, she'll wish she hadn't.

Clarin wiped her tears away. God, she prayed, we have to rescue her. Help us find a way.

Deciding to adopt Anna was easy. Bringing her home however, would be anything but. The cost of adopting her could be more than twenty thousand dollars! But Michelle and her husband (the friends who had already adopted a Russian boy) were spreading the word that Clarin and Paul needed help.

So as Paul and the kids did odd jobs to raise money, donations poured into the adoption agency. Friends stopped by, too. "For Anna," they'd say handing her an envelope.

The family was grateful. But by summer's end, they only had a quarter of what they'd need. What more can we do? Clarin asked herself. Anna's life depended on them.

Meanwhile, Clarin and Paul rushed to

complete the required mountain of paper-
work, while Paul also studied Russian and
taught it to the kids.

And one night, Clarin, Paul and all the
children sat around a tape recorder. "Anna,
this is Mama," Clarin said, first in English,
then in Russian. "This is Papa," Paul began.
"Syestra Kristal," Kristal said, beaming.
"Sister." One by one, each of them introduced themselves. Then they sang a song
they'd made up, "Hello, hello, we're glad
you came to join our family. . . ."

They sent the tape to Orphanage No. 40,
where Clarin pictured a little girl listening
to it again and again, repeating the new
words and the names belonging to the new
voices.

Back in the United States, more donations
poured in. But by October, they were still
thousands of dollars short.

"You can have my frequent flier miles,"
neighbors said. "Let me know if you need a
loan," friends urged.

In the face of such generosity, Clarin
wept with gratitude. Even the Russian gov-
ernment waived some fees.

Finally, they reached the required amount.

"We did it!" they cried. "Anna, we're on our way!"

In nervous excitement, they flew to St. Petersburg, where Clarin and Paul sat in the waiting area at the orphanage, their hearts beating wildly. The door opened.

Tears sprang to Clarin's eyes as a beautiful little girl entered, her arms extended, searching. "Mama! Papa!" she called.

In an instant, Clarin and Paul had taken her into their arms. Anna traced her fingers over their hair and faces. "Hello, hello," she hummed the tune she'd heard on the cassette tape.

"Mama and Papa are finally here, Anna," Clarin whispered. "We're your home now and forever."

At home, Anna's new brothers and sisters introduced themselves. Allyson scooped Anna up in a warm hug and the little girl wrapped her arms and legs around her big sister. "Sistonka, my sister," she cried happily. All the other children took turns hugging her. Brian, who had drilled himself with Russian flash cards, managed to say in Russian, "Hello, my name is Brian." Minutes later, Anna was skipping gaily down the hall with them.

Today, Anna is thriving. Russian words are slowly being replaced with English ones. And the two Clarin hears most these days are, "by myself."

Kristal, who shares her room with Anna, has taught her to play with dolls and have little tea parties. If five-year-old Stephen cries, she will dash over to "love him better." Often, she will sing Russian folk songs in a lilting voice and get lots of hugs when she bows at the end.

In fact, the little Russian girl has adjusted to her new family so quickly that for Clarin, there is only one explanation: Although she was born half a world away, Anna belongs with them.

Marilyn Neibergall
Excerpted from Woman's World

My Mother's Face in the Mirror

Our mothers are racked with the pains of our physical birth; we ourselves suffer the longer pains of our spiritual growth.

MARY ANTIN

"You look just like your mommy."

I couldn't have been more than three or four years old the first time I heard someone say it. I'll never forget the feeling of pride as it welled up inside my tiny chest at the mere notion that someone thought I resembled my mommy.

After that, for a while, I stood a little taller.

Gentle. Soft. Kind. Loving. Beautiful. These are my earliest recollections of my mother. Yet as I grew older, I grew less elated about looking like her.

I must have heard it a million times: "You look just like your mom." By the time I was eight, I equated my mom with a stifling barrier standing between the "me" I was forced to be and the "me" I wanted to be. I began to hate those six words.

By the time I was ready to cross the threshold into puberty, when someone mentioned the likeness, I wanted to scream, "Nooooo! I don't look like her! I look like ME!"

When I moved away from home, our relationship could only be called turbulent. Over the next thirty years, our lone commonality was the certainty of our differences; at the crux of those differences were evidence of the generation gap, as well as some of the world's most "significant" troubles.

For example, in the 1960s, while I was gaga over Tom Jones, Mom clung to her conviction that Bing Crosby was the greatest singer the world had ever known. In the seventies, when women's roles were evolving from traditional housewives into independent entities responsible for their own livelihood and happiness, Mom and I were at odds over what she considered my cavalier interest in finding a man to "take care of me." In the eighties, when I financed three trips to Europe, she admonished me for squandering "a small fortune" on travel expenses instead of investing it in a retirement plan. And finally in the early 1990s, we bickered constantly over the proper way to raise my new son.

"That baby needs to be on a schedule!" she'd insist.

"He's hungry now," I'd respond defensively.

Throughout those years, if she said, "Black," I'd say, "White."

If I said, "Black," she'd say, "White."

And so it went.

Our relationship revolved around superficial issues. Too bad we dealt with them like children. Bickering, nitpicking and competing.

Never in all those years did the thought occur to me—and I'm sure it didn't occur to Mom, either—that a time was approaching when we would be forced to cast aside our differences and respond to one another with mutual respect and to demonstrate the love undeniably ingrained deep in our hearts.

That time came when she was diagnosed with cancer, a deadly variety at an advanced stage. Then everything changed. There would be no more bickering. No more nitpicking. No more competition. There wasn't time. And I realized there had never been time.

Posted at her hospital bedside during her last five months, I watched her grow weaker and sicker as layer upon layer of the protective coating that shielded her most private vulnerabilities was stripped away. I came to understand what an incredibly messy ordeal dying is—chemotherapy, dialysis, being poked and prodded, bleeding, swelling, deteriorating and even suffering from dementia caused by improperly prescribed medications. Yet through it all, my mother maintained her pride and her dignity—two very important qualities I had arrogantly overlooked in all those years of squabbling.

As the clock measuring her life approached the twelve o'clock hour, we made our peace and I rediscovered the beauty, gentleness and kindness of the woman I was so proud to resemble so long ago.

"Mom, I'm here," I had said to her upon my arrival around noon of the day before she died. I am certain, even though a veil of pain-numbing medications shrouded her senses, she knew I was there. She nodded ever so slightly.

But then she stopped responding.

I stayed at her bedside all that night. Except for her arduous breathing, the monotonous gurgling of her oxygen filter and the sporadic beeping of the machines to which she was attached, the hospital room was still. The half-lit fluorescent wall fixture above the bed emitted a surreal illumination that was relaxing in spite of the critical urgency of the moment. I was propped up in a chair next to the bed, alternating between nodding off and waking up every few minutes. When I checked the clock, it registered five o'clock. Mom's breathing was labored and shallow, but no different than it had been for hours. I meant to stay alert, but I couldn't help drifting off again.

At forty minutes past five, shortly before sunrise on Valentine's Day, I awoke. The machines were still beeping, the oxygen was gurgling, but from Mom came only silence. And that's how she slipped away. Quietly, while I slept.

I like to think that as she shed the tired, worn-out shell lying in the bed, she felt whole again. And free of pain. And that before she crossed over to the other side, she took a last look at me and saw the traces of herself that she was leaving behind.

I like to think she knew that my feelings for her had come full circle.

Four years have passed, and I still miss her so. She visits me sometimes in my dreams and assures me she is still nearby. It's immensely comforting. But I have found that when I want to see her, I don't have to wait for sleep. I can simply turn to the closest mirror. The reflection looking back at me may be mine . . . but the face is my mother's.

I see that, and I stand a little taller.

Janis Thornton

A Forgiving Heart

Forgiveness is a gift you give yourself.
SUZANNE SOMERS

This morning, I was in a hurry to get home after running some errands. As I made the right turn into my neighborhood, which is slightly obscured by shrubs, a small boy in a bright yellow T-shirt flashed across the street in front of my car. He stood on the pedals of his red bike, legs pumping, oblivious to me—or any other danger— secure in a boy's invincible immortality.

He passed inches, literally, from my front bumper. I slammed on my brakes, a mean- ingless physical reflex since he was already long gone. I was shaking, and it took a minute to catch my breath. In one terrible instant, that boy's life surely could have ended. His parents would have been in pain forever, and my own life would have been a nightmare.

I continued down the street, recalling the image of the boy's face. Magnified by my fright, I could clearly picture his eyes wide with a dazzling mix of bravado and fear, a bright haughty smile lit by yet another triumph over the dull world of adult concern. He was so startlingly energetic, so fearless that my shock at very nearly killing him was almost immediately replaced by anger bordering on fury.

Churning with rage—at his carelessness, not mine—I went home. The agitation my near-miss brought upon me troubled me most of the day. Then, at twilight, I remembered Mikey.

Growing up, Mike Roberts was my best buddy. My father was a doctor in a small Ohio River town, and my parents and Mike's parents were close friends. In fact, his house was one vacant lot away from my father's clinic.

Mikey, as we all called him, was adventurous

and daring. His mother, Judy, was easy on us kids and made the best peanut butter cookies in the universe. They never locked their doors, and I had the run of their house.

One Friday, my mother planned to go to Cincinnati to shop and told me I should spend the day at the Roberts's house. Judy was expecting me. I was not to eat too many cookies or ride my bike in the road.

When my mother left that morning, I set off on my bike to the Roberts's house. I was about fifty yards from the turn that led to Mikey's street when I heard a sound that I can still hear sometimes in dreams. It was the fierce squeal of tires when you put on the brakes really hard. It seemed to last for a very long time, although I am sure, in retrospect, that the noise died quickly. And then there was the harsh sound of metal crushing. In a flash, I took off on my bike and rounded the corner at full speed.

There was a truck in the road, turned almost sideways. Beyond the front fender was Mikey's red Schwinn, folded so that it seemed to be just half a bike, two tires now flattened against each other.

Mikey was lying on the grass, a great hulk

of a man bent over him. I got off my bike, dropped it, and ran to where my friend lay, silent and still on a carpet of leaves. At that instant, the front door of his house opened and his mother came out. I don't think I have ever seen anyone run so fast. At the same time, a gurney appeared from my father's clinic followed by my dad and an orderly.

Instantly, there was quite a crowd. Judy knelt at Mikey's head and passed her hand gently over his forehead. My father told Judy not to move her son and bent to examine him. The truck driver sat down heavily a few feet away. He must have weighed over two hundred pounds. He had great round shoulders and a thick neck that had deep circles of wrinkles that shone with sweat. He had on blue coveralls and a red plaid shirt.

Now he sat on the grass like some stunned bull. His head rested on his drawn-up knees and his shoulders shook, but I don't think he was crying.

I stared at the man, trying to make him feel how mad I was. He had probably not been paying attention, I thought. Not an unfamiliar failing among the adults I knew. They often seemed careless to me, and this one had hurt my friend. I wanted to hurt him back in some terrible way.

In a few minutes, Mikey was awake and crying. My father had him immobilized on a stretcher board and loaded onto the gurney. Judy held Mikey's hand, and they all moved away into the clinic's emergency entrance. I was left alone with the trucker who was now sitting with his head bowed on his crossed arms. His body was still shaking like he had a chill.

We sat in silence for what seemed a long time. Then Judy came out of the clinic's front entrance and walked over to us. She said that Mikey would be fine. It was only his arm. It could have been much worse.

I thought she surely would slap the driver or at least give him a severe talking to. But what she actually did astonished me. She told him to come with her into her house. "And you, too," she said to me.

She asked the driver his name him to sit by the fireplace and she some coffee. He raised his hand to off but she brought coffee anyway, a and cookies for me. Stan, the driver, couldn't eat or drink. He sat in the blue arm-chair, filling it completely. From time to time, he would shake and Judy would put her arm around his shoulder and talk to him in her wonderful gentle voice, "It's not your fault. You weren't speeding. Mikey takes stupid risks, and I am so sorry about that. I'm just grateful he wasn't hurt badly. And I don't blame you. You shouldn't blame your-self, either."

I listened to her incredulously. How could she say such things to the man who'd nearly killed her son, my friend? What was the matter with her? Before long, she got the driver sort of put back together—at least that's how it looked to me—and he got up to leave.

As he reached the door he turned to her and said, "I have a boy, too. I know what it took for you to help me."

Then, to add one more astonishment to the day, Judy stood on tiptoe and kissed him on the cheek.

I had never been able to understand how Judy could offer ease and comfort to a man who had very nearly killed her child . . .

until today, when I turned the corner into my familiar neighborhood and came within inches of what surely would have been a terrible and irreversible act.

Still trying to shake the dread that had occupied my mind all day, I thought of Mikey's mother and that day in a long-ago autumn. And although there was no one there to comfort me, to tell me that I had not been at fault, that bad things do happen no matter how careful you are, the memory of that day reached across time to help me.

That one mother's empathy, like all other gifts of goodness, had never left the world, and it could be called upon to console and heal. And would continue to do so . . . perhaps forever.

W. W. Meade

The Miracle Baby

Faith is being sure of what we hope for and certain of what we do not see.

HEBREWS 11:1

He was born six and a half weeks prematurely on a hot, August day in 1967 and was quickly whisked away to a waiting incubator. At a mere four pounds, eleven ounces, and looking like a partially inflated doll, he was still the most beautiful baby she had ever seen.

The baby's father, Dr. Carter,* tried to tell his wife, Donna, not to expect too much— their baby was severely jaundiced. More than anything in the world, he had wanted to tell her their little baby was just fine,

*Names have been changed throughout the story to protect privacy.

especially after three miscarriages, and all the sadness they'd felt and tears they shed. But their baby wasn't fine.

In spite of all his medical training and experience, Dr. Carter choked on the words. But he knew he'd have to tell her that the baby they had wanted so badly for years was probably not going to live—maybe forty-eight hours at the most. He had to prepare her for what was to come.

She immediately named the baby Jeffrey, after her husband. As the baby's jaundice grew worse, fellow physicians came by to console them. They shook their heads and tried their best to offer some encouragement. But they knew the odds were not good. Even if he lived, unless little Jeffrey's liver began functioning soon, the jaundice would produce permanent brain damage.

Donna told everyone he was going to be all right. She knew her baby was going to live. The nurses felt sorry for her since her baby was probably going to die anyway, and so they let her hold him. When she touched his tiny, fragile body and whispered that he was going to grow up to be a strong, healthy man, little Jeffrey smiled.

She told the nurses what had happened, and they looked at her sadly and said that babies have involuntary smiles and she needed rest. They did not have the heart to tell her more.

The extended family discussed burial arrangements with her husband and the parish priest. They finally came in to speak with Donna. She started crying and asked everyone to leave the hospital room. Her baby was not going to be buried. He was going to go home, jaundiced or not. She would not even think of burial!

At sixty-two hours, the baby's blood count was checked again. The jaundice was considerably better! Little Jeffrey began eating every two hours. Donna asked to hold him as much as possible, and she talked to him. Since he didn't need oxygen, the nurses humored her. At the next check, the count had dropped another two points. Donna began planning his homecoming party.

Jeffrey did go home almost three weeks after birth. That, however, was not the end of the story.

Six weeks later, at his first checkup, the pediatrician told Donna he thought the baby was possibly blind or had eye damage. She said this was nonsense since he followed her with his eyes. After a few tests, it proved to be a false scare. Yet, the first year, the baby did not do much. He had routine checkups, but Donna knew he seemed far behind in his development. Had he suffered severe brain damage from the jaundice?

At thirteen months Jeffrey suddenly had a small seizure. They rushed him to the hospital, and he was diagnosed with a possible brain tumor. After several tests and X rays the neurologist said Jeffrey was hydrocephalic (water on the brain), and they would have to operate immediately to put a permanent shunt inside his head. At this time, a shunt operation was still rather experimental. It was the only procedure known to keep these children alive.

Once again, Donna did not fully accept the diagnosis. If he was hydrocephalic, why did it just now develop? Her friends told her she was in denial. She'd better listen to the doctors.

Of course, she would do whatever was necessary to help her son, but she also made her own plan of action. Three days before the operation, she called everyone she knew in several states and asked them to pray at 7:00 P.M. each night before the operation. She asked them to ask others to join them if they could.

When the operation day arrived, she felt calm. Friends in seven states had been praying for their son. Later, to her astonishment she learned that her friends had called people, who then called other people, and that ultimately hundreds of people had been gathered to pray at 7:00 P.M. on three successive nights. Even a group of people in Israel were among those praying! And all for a tiny child none of them even knew!

The operation started very early. Donna and her husband paced the floors of the hospital. After what seemed only a short time, the neurosurgeon came running out, wildly waving X rays. He was grinning from ear to ear. "It's a miracle! We didn't have to do anything. We did the last test through the baby's soft spot, and there was nothing there. He is not hydrocephalic!"

They all started to cry and laugh at the same time. The neurosurgeon said he did not know what to think. He had no explanation for it.

So Jeffrey came home once again to a

jubilant crowd of friends and family. All the people who prayed for him were notified of the results and thanked for their prayers. He never had another seizure again.

Still, according to everyone else's timetable, his development was very slow. At Jeffrey's three-year pediatric checkup, the doctor looked sternly at Donna and asked if she and her husband had given thought to institutionalizing him. Donna was stunned. Institutionalize him? How could anyone do that? She refused, and it was never discussed again.

Instead, Donna set up the family basement playroom like a Montessori school. Jeffrey wasn't really learning language so she worked with him by engaging learning techniques that involved all his senses— sight, smell, touch, taste and hearing. Donna believed Jeffrey was normal and just didn't follow other people's timetables.

She taught him colors using M&Ms. He quickly learned the names of colors and of other things, too. And, while not speaking much more than a few words here and there until he was three and a half years old, his first full sentence was "Pass the ketchup!"

He progressed quickly when he learned anything new—not little by little as his sister did, but in giant spurts, all-at-once kind of steps. This became a pattern in his life.

When Jeffrey was four, Donna wanted him to go to real preschool just like his sister. The first year he played with the water fountain—all year. He turned the water off and on, endlessly. The teachers said it was a waste of money to send him to school. He would be better off in "special school." They said he was "slow," and one teacher in exasperation said that Jeffrey was retarded and she ought to know—she'd been teaching for twenty-five years!

Donna remained firm. Would they mind as long as she was paying for it, to keep him another year? They reluctantly agreed but only if he was not allowed to play with the water fountain. She agreed to the terms.

The next fall he began preschool again. This time he began building intricate architectural structures. He also began examining all the plastic dinosaurs and knew their names, classifying them by types. He found new interests in doing the math blocks, talking and asking question after question after question. He was more social and didn't play with the water fountain. The teachers couldn't believe it. He actually seemed bright!

However, at his pediatric checkup, his new doctor said he thought Jeffrey needed testing. He felt he had developmental delays. After testing, the pediatrician, who is now distinguished nationally in his field, said Jeffrey was autistic. Donna decided she'd had enough! Since birth, Jeffrey had been "diagnosed" as possibly (1) blind, (2) hydrocephalic, (3) epileptic, (4) retarded and now finally (5) autistic. If she and her husband had listened to experts, well-meaning friends and even some family members, Jeffrey would be in an institution. Donna was polite but said that she did not think Jeffrey was autistic at all. He was in preschool and was going to start first grade on time.

Other than being very uncoordinated and not having well-developed motor skills, Jeffrey's elementary years were not unusual. His learning ability was completely on track. He became an Eagle Scout, an honor student, a presidential scholar in his senior year, won two academic scholarships for college and was in all gifted classes. His SAT scores shocked everyone.

But even this is not the end of the story.

After graduating from college with honors, Jeffrey was encouraged to go to medical school. Donna always told him she had faith that his life had a special purpose and that he was here to help people. After graduating medical school, Jeffrey was accepted at a prestigious clinic for his residency program.

One day, while he was doing a rotation in the emergency room, an older man burst in. He was suicidal and, as a last-ditch effort, one of his friends had brought him in to talk to someone. Jeffrey saw him and asked about his life. The man told him about how sad he was about his recent divorce and being downsized out of a job he had held for years. He felt hopeless, that his life was over and nothing he had done had mattered. Jeffrey talked to him a while and, after giving him some tests, gave him a prescription that would help him for the next few days. Jeffrey also got him approved for a caseworker to follow him up for the next month.

Suddenly the patient looked at the doctor's badge and said, "Jeffrey Carter? Is your mom's name Donna?"

Jeffrey answered, "Why, yes. How did you know?"

"You're the miracle baby! You're the miracle baby!" the man cried excitedly. "I prayed for you when you were in the hospital, and now you're a doctor!"

Jeffrey confirmed that he had been born in Minnesota and now he'd returned "home" to complete his medical training.

The old man smiled and just gazed at his new doctor as if examining every inch. Then he told Jeffrey the story.

"Were you really one of the people who prayed for me?" Jeffrey asked him.

"Oh yes, three nights a week at 7:00 P.M. for years. We were only supposed to do it until the operation, but some of us just kept going for a while."

"You prayed for me all that time?"

As the man nodded, tears began to form in his eyes. Jeffrey reached out to embrace his patient—a man who only hours before had thought of taking his own life because he had lost all faith.

"Thank you, for praying for me . . . for caring about me. You see, I'm here because of you."

Faith had come full circle for both men.

Ronna Rowlette

Leaving Home

It's always been my feeling that God lends you your children until they're about eighteen years old. If you haven't made your points with them by then, it's too late.

BETTY FORD

"I'm not going to cry," I told my husband, Chuck, as we left the parent-orientation session held several months before our daughter would attend college in the fall.

Maybe those other mothers were going to cry after dropping off their kids at the dorm, but not me. I looked around the auditorium at the other mothers, wondering which ones were going to be crybabies. I thought, I won't clutch a box of tissues when the time comes to say good-bye to

Sarah. I'm from sturdier stock than that. Why snivel and sob just because my little girl is growing up?

We'd spent the afternoon listening to parents of upperclassmen talk about how our lives were going to change when our children left home for college. One seasoned mother warned that we would cry all the way home.

I elbowed Chuck. "That's ridiculous," I said. "Why are they making such a big deal out of this?" Being a mother has always been important to me, but—for crying out loud—it isn't the only thing! I have a job, I have friends, I have a life!

Sarah and I spent the summer sniping at each other. I hated the way she talked about how she couldn't wait to leave—as if her life at home with us had been some kind of hostage standoff. She hated the way I nagged her about cleaning up her room and putting her dishes in the sink, the way I grumbled when I needed to use the phone and she was tying up the line, the way I questioned her whereabouts when she went out with her friends. After all, she was eighteen. She didn't need to check in with her mom every five minutes.

In August, I ran into my friend, Pat, at the library. Pat remembered the weeks before her daughter left home for college the previous year.

"We fought all summer long," she said. "I think it was our way of getting used to the idea of living apart. When you're arguing all the time and angry, then you don't feel so bad about her leaving."

"And," I responded thoughtfully, "she doesn't feel so bad about leaving when she's mad at Mom."

On moving day, we helped her unpack and store her belongings in the dorm room. I tucked the extra-long twin sheets onto Sarah's mattress while Chuck assembled a storage shelf for her closet. After lunch, we said good-bye, hugged at the curb, and then Chuck and I drove away.

The woman at the parent-orientation session was wrong, I thought. This isn't so bad.

Two days later I walked by her bedroom. The door was open, her bed was made and all the clutter of her childhood, of her teenage years, was missing. Suddenly, it dawned on me: She's gone.

Later, as I was vacuuming in the living room, I thought I heard someone say, "Mom," and I turned off the vacuum cleaner to listen for footsteps coming through the door, to answer a child's call. Then I realized I was alone in the house. Sarah was gone, and nothing would ever be the same.

I longed to hear her voice. I wanted to know what she was doing. I wanted her to sit on the edge of my bed at night like she used to and tell me about her day, her classes, her teachers, her friends, the boys she liked, the boys who liked her. . . .

"What's wrong?" Chuck asked when he came home. I was chopping vegetables for stir-fry. He peered into my face. "Are you crying?"

"It's just the onions," I sniffed as a tear snaked down my cheek.

After dinner I said, "Let's call her. Maybe she's expecting us to call."

"It's only been two days," Chuck said. "Let's give her at least a week to settle in."

He was right, of course. I didn't want to turn into some kind of Stalker Mom. I remembered what it was like to be eighteen and away from home for the first time. She was meeting new friends, learning new ideas, forming new bonds. I had to give her the space—the distance—she needed.

Then the phone rang.

"Hi, Mom," Sarah said. "Could you send me some pictures to put on my bulletin board? And a few stuffed animals?"

She wanted her teddy bear. She wanted a photo of her father and me—and one of her younger brother. She loved being at school, but she missed us, too. And then she started telling me about her day, her classes, her teachers, her friends, the boys she liked, the boys who liked her. . . .

Beth Copeland Vargo

Chocolate-Covered Cherries

[EDITORS' NOTE: *This Christmas letter was sent to friends and family along with a box of chocolate-covered cherries.*]

What a terrible way to spend Christmas! My oldest son, Cameron, had been diagnosed with acute myeloblastic leukemia the previous June. After a harrowing ride in a military helicopter to Walter Reed Hospital, three rounds of horrendous chemotherapy, an excruciating lung resection, and a disappointing bone marrow search, we were at Duke University Hospital. Cameron had undergone a cord blood transplant, a last-ditch effort to save his life, in early December. Now, here it was Christmas Eve.

Spending Christmas in the small room on Ward 9200 seemed strange—so different from our usual holiday setting at home. We had always spent weeks on our favorite holiday project: baking cookies. Now the cookies were sent from family and friends, since I tried to spend all my time with Cameron, helping to ease the long, tedious hours. He had been in isolation for weeks, because the chemotherapy and drugs they used to make his new bone marrow engraft left him with no immune system. When presents had arrived in the mail, we hadn't waited for Christmas, but had opened them immediately—anything to create a bright moment in that dull and painful time.

Always in the past, 6:00 P.M. on Christmas Eve was the "Magic Hour." This was the time when everyone in my family, in Iowa, Wisconsin, California and Washington, D.C., opened our presents. We all did this at exactly the same time, somehow bringing the family together, even though we lived so far apart. Cameron's father, stepmother, sister and brother also opened presents at their house at that time.

This year, the Magic Hour would find just Cameron and me in a small, almost-bare hospital room, since most decorations weren't allowed in the sterile environment.

We sat together, listening to the drone of the HEPA filter and the beeping of the six infusion pumps hooked to a catheter in his heart, as Cameron waited until 6:00 P.M. . . . exactly, to open the few presents I had saved aside for him. He insisted we follow this small tradition, to create some semblance of normalcy—all of which had been abruptly abandoned six months earlier. I watched him open the presents. His favorite was a Hug Me Elmo toy that said, "I love you," when you squeezed it.

All too quickly, Christmas was over. Or so I thought.

Cameron carefully reached over the side of his hospital bed and handed me a small green box. It was wrapped beautifully, obviously by a gift store, with perfect edges and a folded piece of ribbon held down with a gold embossed sticker.

Surprised, I said, "For me?"

"Mom, it wouldn't be Christmas unless you have something to unwrap, too," he replied.

For a moment, I was speechless. Finally I asked, "But, how did you get this? Did you ask a nurse to run down to the gift store?"

Cameron leaned back in his bed, and gave me his most devilish smile. "Nope. Yesterday, when you went home for a few hours to take a shower, I sneaked downstairs."

"CAMERON! You aren't supposed to leave the floor! You know you're susceptible to almost any germ. They let you leave the ward?"

"Nope!" His smile was even bigger now. "They weren't looking. I just walked out."

This was no small feat, because since the cord blood transplant, Cameron had grown weaker. He could barely walk, and certainly not unassisted. It took every ounce of strength just to cruise the small ward halls, pushing the heavy IV pole hung with medication and a pain pump. How could he possibly have made it nine floors to the gift store?

"Don't worry, Mom. I wore my mask, and I used the cane. Man, they really chewed me out when I got back. I couldn't sneak back in, since they'd been looking for me."

I couldn't look up. I held the box even tighter now and had already started to cry.

"Open it! It's not much, but it wouldn't be Christmas if you didn't have something from me to unwrap."

I opened the box of gift-store-wrapped chocolate-covered cherries. "They are your favorite, right?" he asked hopefully.

I finally looked at my poor eighteen-year-old baby. Cameron had begun all this suffering almost immediately after his high school graduation. Did he know how much he was teaching me about what being a family really meant? "Oh, absolutely my favorite!"

Cameron chuckled a little bit, "See, we still have our traditions—even in here."

"Cameron, this is the best present I've ever received . . . ever," I told him, and I meant every word. "Let's start a new tradition. Every Christmas, let's only give each other a box of chocolate-covered cherries, and we'll reminisce about the year we spent Christmas at Duke University Hospital battling leukemia. We'll remember how horrible it all was and how glad we are that it is finally over."

We made that pact right then and there, as we shared the box of chocolate-covered cherries. What a wonderful way to spend Christmas!

Cameron died two months later, after two unsuccessful cord blood transplants. He was so brave—never giving in, never giving up. This will be my first Christmas without him and the first Christmas without something from him to unwrap.

This is my gift to you. A box of chocolate-covered cherries. And when you open it, I hope it will remind you what the holidays are really about . . . being with your friends and family . . . recreating traditions, maybe starting some new ones . . . but most of all—love.

What a beautiful way to spend Christmas.

Dawn Holt

"They don't come with a
snooze button, Steven."

Who Is Jack Canfield?

Jack Canfield is one of America's leading experts in the development of human potential and personal effectiveness. He is both a dynamic, entertaining speaker and a highly sought-after trainer. Jack has a wonderful ability to inform and inspire audiences toward increased levels of self-esteem and peak performance.

In addition to the *Chicken Soup for the Soul* series, Jack has coauthored numerous books, including his most recent release, *The Success Principles, How to Get From Where You Are to Where You Want to Be* with Janet Switzer, *The Aladdin Factor* with Mark Victor Hansen, *100 Ways to Build Self-Concept in the Classroom* with Harold C. Wells, *Heart at Work* with Jacqueline Miller and *The Power of Focus* with Les Hewitt and Mark Victor Hansen.

Jack is regularly seen on television shows such as Good Morning America, 20/20 and NBC Nightly News.

For further information about Jack's books, tapes and training programs, or to schedule him for a presentation, please contact:

Self-Esteem Seminars
P.O. Box 30880
Santa Barbara, CA 93130
Phone: 805-563-2935
Fax: 805-563-2945
Web: *www.chickensoup.com*

Who Is Mark Victor Hansen?

In the area of human potential, no one is better known and more respected than Mark Victor Hansen. For more than thirty years, Mark has focused solely on helping people from all walks of life reshape their personal vision of what's possible. .

He is a sought-after keynote speaker, bestselling author and marketing maven. Mark is a prolific writer with many bestselling books such as *The One Minute Millionaire*, *The Power of Focus*, *The Aladdin Factor* and *Dare to Win*, in addition to the *Chicken Soup for the Soul* series.

Mark has appeared on Oprah, CNN and The Today Show, and has been featured in *Time, U.S. News & World Report, USA Today, New York Times* and *Entrepreneur* and countless radio and newspaper interviews.

As a passionate philanthropist and humanitarian, he has been the recipient of numerous awards that honor his entrepreneurial spirit, philanthropic heart and business acumen.

For further information on Mark's products and services, please contact:

Mark Victor Hansen & Associates, Inc.
P.O. Box 7665
Newport Beach, CA 92658
Phone: 949-764-2640
Fax: 949-722-6912
FREE resources online at:
www.markvictorhansen.com

Who Is Marci Shimoff?

Marci Shimoff is coauthor of the *New York Times* bestsellers *Chicken Soup for the Woman's Soul, Chicken Soup for the Mother's Soul, A Second Chicken Soup for the Woman's Soul, Chicken Soup for the Single's Soul.* She is a top-rated professional speaker who, for the last eighteen years, has inspired thousands of people with her message of personal and professional growth. Since 1994 she has specialized in delivering *Chicken Soup for the Soul* keynote speeches to audiences around the world.

Marci is cofounder and president of The Esteem Group, a company specializing in self-esteem and inspirational programs for women. She has been a featured speaker for numerous professional organizations, universities, women's associations, healthcare organizations and Fortune 500 companies. Her clients have included AT&T, American Airlines, Sears, Junior League, the Pampered Chef, Jazzercise and Bristol-Myers Squibb. Her audiences appreciate her lively humor, her dynamic delivery and her ability to open hearts and uplift spirits.

To schedule Marci for a *Chicken Soup for the Soul* keynote address or seminar, you can reach her at:

The Esteem Group
191 Bayview Drive
San Rafael, CA 94901
phone: 415-789-1300 • fax: 415-789-1309

Who Is Carol Kline?

Carol Kline is a speaker, self-esteem facilitator and certified instructor of the parenting skills program, Redirecting Children's Behavior (RCB).Carol has offered workshops, weekly classes for parents and in-service programs for child-care providers since 1993. Since 1975, Carol has also taught stress-management programs to the general public.

In 1990, she began studying the area of self-esteem with Jack Canfield and has assisted as a facilitator in his annual Train the Trainers program. Her dynamic and engaging style has won her enthusiastic receptions from the various audiences she addresses.

In addition to her parenting, self-esteem and volunteer work, Carol has been a freelance writer for fourteen years. Carol, who has a B.A. in literature, has written for newspapers, newsletters and other publications. She has presented seminars for writers on effective story writing and has spoken at writing conferences around the country. She is the coauthor of the *New York Times* best-selling *Chicken Soup for the Pet Lover's Soul* and *Chicken Soup for the Cat and Dog Lover's Soul.* She has also contributed stories and her editing talents to many other *Chicken Soup for the Soul* books.

To contact Carol:
P.O. Box 1262
Fairfield, IA 52556
Phone: 641-469-3889 • Fax: 641-472-3720
E-mail: *motherschickensoup@yahoo.com*

Contributors

If you would like to contact any of the contributors for information about their writing or would like to invite them to speak in your community, look for their contact information included in their biography.

Martha Campbell is a graduate of Washington University St. Louis School of Fine Arts, and a former writer/designer for Hallmark Cards. She has been a freelance cartoonist and book illustrator since 1973. She can be reached at P.O. Box 2538, Harrison, AR 72602, 870-741-5323, or *marthaf@alltel.net.*

Lisa Duffy-Korpics is a freelance writer and high school social studies teacher in Montgomery, New York. Her work has appeared in magazines and regional newspapers, as well as in *Chicken Soup for the Cat and Dog Lover's Soul.* Lisa lives in Dutchess County, New York, with her husband Jason, her six-year-old son Charles and three-year-old daughter Emily. Her mother, Kathleen, is currently on her twenty-eighth year of dialysis. Lisa can be reached at *Memleigh@msn.com.*

Falaka Fattah is the founder and Chief Executive Officer of the House of Umoja in Philadelphia, a home established almost thirty years ago for troubled urban youth. When asked once how she managed to convert the boys under her care into such well-behaved young men, she responded, "I treat them with respect, I demand that they respect me and I love them with an unconditional love." To make a tax-deductible donation, please send checks to: House of Umoja, Inc., 1410 N. Frazier St., Philadelphia, PA 19131. Or contact Mrs.

Fattah at (215) 473-5893, Fax: (215) 879-5340, e-mail: *falakafattah@aol.com.*

Karie Hansen is a single mother and a full-time student studying Elementary Education in Iowa. Her inspiration for writing is her daughter Loreena.

Dawn Holt is currently a school counselor at Westover High School in Fayetteville, North Carolina, fulfilling her son Cameron's last wishes that he not be forgotten, and that she come back to his high school to make a difference in the lives of the students. After giving the chocolate-covered cherries story to family and friends in December of 1998, they encouraged her to submit the story to *Chicken Soup for the Soul.* She still makes the box of candy her annual gift to them.

Scott Masear lives in Portland, Oregon, and has been cartooning professionally for fifteen years. Some of the magazines that he sells to regularly are *Harvard Business Review, Medical Economics, Air and Space, Phi Delta Kappa, National Law Journal* and *Travel Weekly.*

W. W. Meade's first story was published in *Colliers* magazine when he was twenty-two. He wrote short fiction stories for the *Saturday Evening Post, Gentleman's Quarterly* and several others. He then turned to writing nonfiction for magazines such as *Cosmopolitan, Redbook* and *Reader's Digest.* Later he became the managing editor of *Cosmopolitan* and then the managing editor of the Reader's Digest Book Club. His last position in publishing was president and editor in chief of Avon Books. Today, Walter is retired and writing short stories for *Reader's Digest* as well as many other magazines and periodicals. He can be reached at 4561 N.W. 67 Terr., Fort Lauderhill, FL 33319.

Marilyn Neibergall holds a Bachelor of Science Degree in Nursing from Arizona State University and is an

R.N.—community health nurse—at Maricopa County
Department of Public Health in Phoenix, Arizona. She is
also a freelance writer with several articles in *Woman's
World* magazine. She can be reached at 1030 W. Emelita
Avenue, Mesa, AZ 85210 or call 480-969-1794.

Ronna Rowlette is the mother of two daughters and a
son. She is president of Rowlette Research Associates,
Inc., in Tampa, Florida, specializing in community
research with nonprofit organizations. Dr. Rowlette is
also an adjunct professor, a freelance writer and photog-
rapher.

Janis Thornton lives in Tipton, Indiana. A staff writer for
the *Frankfort* (Ind.) *Times,* she also operates a writing and
graphic design service from her home. A part-time student at Indiana University, Janis is continuing her studies in creative writing. Her "mother's soul" is nourished
daily by her eleven-year-old son, Matthew.

Beth Copeland Vargo is a museum curator, freelance
writer and poet. Her poetry collection, *Traveling Through
Glass*, received the 1999 Bright Hill Press National
Poetry Book Award. She received her M.F.A. degree in
Creative Writing from Bowling Green State University
and has taught writing to children and adults. Her
personal essays have appeared in the *Chicago Tribune,
Christian Science Monitor* and other publications.

Supporting Mothers and Children Around the World

A portion of the proceeds from the sale of each copy of the original edition of *Chicken Soup for the Mother's Soul 2* is donated to the following non-profit organizations. Please contact them directly for more information. We invite you to join us in supporting these organizations:

The **March of Dimes** is dedicated to improving the health of babies by:
- Funding lifesaving research on birth defects and low birthweight.
- Providing expectant parents with the latest scientific information.
- Fighting for health care for all our kids.
- Helping women get quality prenatal care.

For free help or information about pregnancy or birth defects, contact:
March of Dimes
1275 Mamaroneck Ave.
White Plains, NY 10605
Phone: 888-MODIMES (888-663-4637)
Web site: www.modimes.org

Children's Relief Network is dedicated to saving and rehabilitating the lives of abandoned and orphaned street children in Bucharest, Romania. In 1994, Angie Thomson founded the organization after a trip to Bucharest where she found young children left on the streets to survive on their own. Since then, Children's Relief Network has developed The Villa of Hope for Boys, The House of Hope for Girls, The Hope Rescue Center, The Refuge of Hope for Girls, The Hope Orphanage Outreach, and the Village of Hope. Contact:

Children's Relief Network, Int'l.
P.O. Box 668
Deerfield Beach, FL 33443
Phone: 800-326-6500
Web site: www.romanianchildren.org.

The House of Umoja was established in 1968 as a home for troubled urban youth. The unique methods employed by the founders, Dave and Falaka Fattah, have been successful in turning around the lives of thousands of young men. Authorities credit the House of Umoja for playing a major role in eliminating the gang warfare that plagued Philadelphia in the 1970s. Today, the House of Umoja is one of the most acclaimed and successful youth service programs in the country and was selected as a crime prevention model by the Department of Health and Human Services and the Police Foundation. A successful replication of the House of Umoja is in operation in Portland, Oregon. Contact:

The House of Umoja
1410 N. Frazier St.
Philadelphia, PA 19131
Phone: 215-473-5893

The Alliance for Bio-Integrity is dedicated to promoting technologies that foster human and environmental health and addressing the problems of those that do not. The Alliance is dedicated to preserve the safety of our food supply, the health of the environment and the harmony of our relationship with nature. Contact:
The Alliance for Bio-Integrity
Phone: 641-472-5554
Web site: www.biointegrity.org

Humanity in Unity is dedicated to supporting humanitarian and educational projects which address issues of poverty, disease, and inequality. The organization's activities currently include sponsoring inner city programs, funding AIDS facilities, and ministering to women who have suffered abuse or are undergoing rehabilitation. Humanity in Unity is dedicated to improving conditions for women and children, and unifying our world family through bridging economic, social and cultural differences. Contact:
Humanity in Unity
500 Hartford Dr.
Boulder, CO 80305
Phone: 303-554-0880

Homes for Change is a volunteer organization dedicated to building basic, inexpensive, yet durable housing for the poorest families worldwide. Frequent recipients of these homes are women with children, often victims of abuse and neglect, all of whom must work for meager wages simply to survive. Homes for Change provides a foundation for these families to live independently, to grow materially and socially and to become contributing members of their communities. Contact:

Homes for Change
13029 Triadelphia Mill Road
Clarksville, MD 21029
Phone: 301-854-0087

More Chicken Soup?

We enjoy hearing your reactions to the stories in *Chicken Soup for the Soul* books. Please let us know what your favorite stories were and how they affected you.

Many of the stories and poems you enjoy in *Chicken Soup for the Soul* books are submitted by readers like you who had read earlier *Chicken Soup for the Soul* selections.

We invite you to contribute a story to one of these future volumes.

Stories may be up to 1,200 words and must uplift or inspire. To obtain a copy of our submission guidelines and a listing of upcoming *Chicken Soup* books, please write, fax or check our Web sites.

Chicken Soup for the Soul
P.O. Box 30880
Santa Barbara, CA 93130
fax: 805-563-2945
Web site: *www.chickensoup.com*

Guaranteed to make you smile!

Take time for you.

Also Available

Chicken Soup African American Soul
Chicken Soup Body and Soul
Chicken Soup Bride's Soul
Chicken Soup Caregiver's Soul
Chicken Soup Cat and Dog Lover's Soul
Chicken Soup Christian Family Soul
Chicken Soup Christian Soul
Chicken Soup College Soul
Chicken Soup Country Soul
Chicken Soup Couple's Soul
Chicken Soup Expectant Mother's Soul
Chicken Soup Father's Soul
Chicken Soup Fisherman's Soul
Chicken Soup Girlfriend's Soul
Chicken Soup Golden Soul
Chicken Soup Golfer's Soul, Vol. I, II
Chicken Soup Horse Lover's Soul
Chicken Soup Inspire a Woman's Soul
Chicken Soup Kid's Soul
Chicken Soup Mother's Soul, Vol. I, II
Chicken Soup Nature Lover's Soul
Chicken Soup Parent's Soul
Chicken Soup Pet Lover's Soul
Chicken Soup Preteen Soul, Vol. I, II
Chicken Soup Single's Soul
Chicken Soup Soul, Vol. I-VI
Chicken Soup at Work
Chicken Soup Sports Fan's Soul
Chicken Soup Teenage Soul, Vol. I-IV
Chicken Soup Woman's Soul, Vol. I, II

Available wherever books are sold.
For a complete listing or to order direct:
Telephone (800) 441-5569 • Online www.hcibooks.com
Prices do not include shipping and handling. Your response code is CCS.